THE YORKSHIRE COAST

Mark Denton

Mark Denton

Oct. 06.

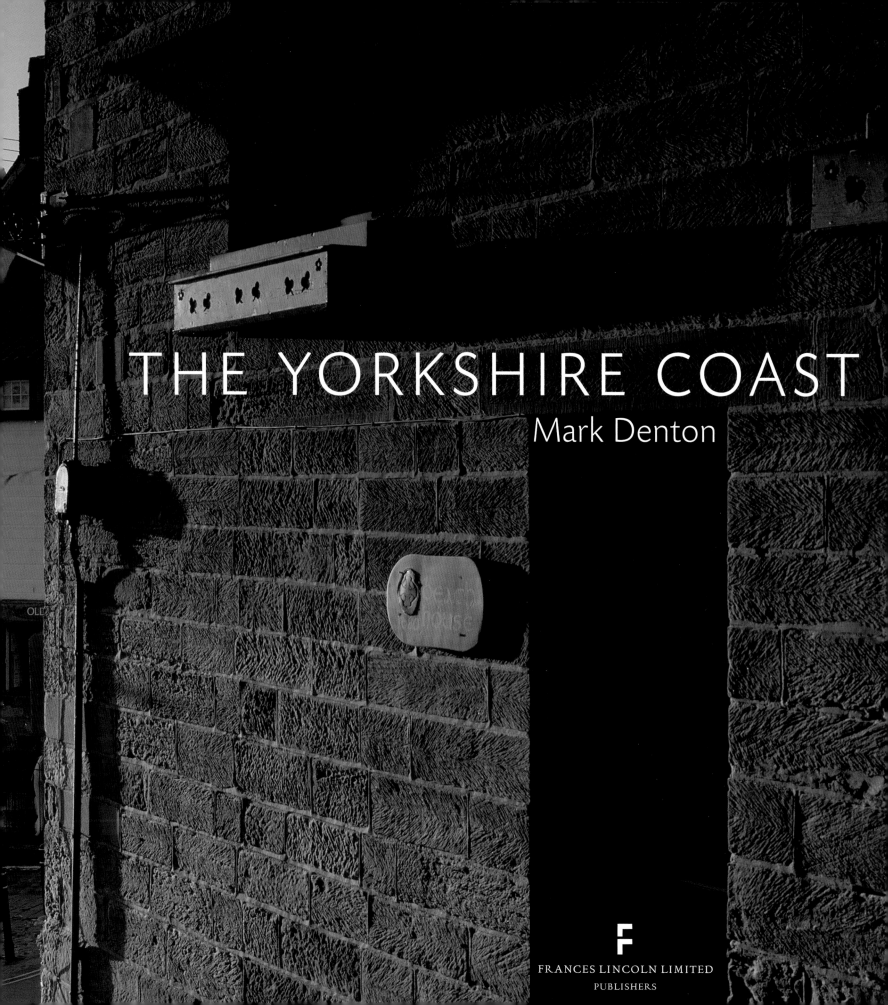

THE YORKSHIRE COAST

Mark Denton

F

FRANCES LINCOLN LIMITED

PUBLISHERS

Frances Lincoln Ltd
4 Torriano Mews
Torriano Avenue
London NW5 2RZ
www.franceslincoln.com

The Yorkshire Coast
Copyright © Frances Lincoln Ltd 2006
Photographs and text copyright © Mark Denton 2006
Additional text copyright © G.P. Taylor 2006

British Library Cataloguing-in-Publication data
A catalogue record for this book is available from the British Library.

ISBN 13: 978-0-7112-2607-4
ISBN 10: 0-7112-2607-5

Printed and bound in Singapore

9 8 7 6 5 4 3 2 1

above
Bright green weed covers a modern slipway on the western
side of Staithes harbour.

half title page
Purple and violet hues gather to warm a bitterly cold
February dawn in Filey Bay. If skies are clear, the rising sun is
visible almost year-round from this six-mile stretch of sand.

title page
Bunting at Robin Hood's Bay heralds the arrival of Christmas
and dawn sunshine highlights one of the many traditional
stone-built fishermen's cottages.

For Rachel and Lucy.
Thank you for your love and support.

CONTENTS

INTRODUCTION

I was always drawn to the coast; it's in my upbringing.

I must admit from the outset that I am not a Yorkshireman. I was raised 500 yards from the North Sea, but in Seaburn, north of the River Wear in Sunderland. A very brief journey nowadays, it seemed rather longer with short legs, but it was always with much energy that I ran excitedly down Dykelands Road to the beach. Digging holes in search of Australia was one of my favourite pastimes; another was throwing stones into the sea. Perhaps at this early age I was already experiencing the feelings of peace and even melancholy that the sea brings me today – a photo taken by my father on the beach shows me at five years old with a very wistful look in my eye. When I acquired my first camera aged around twelve, instinctively my first photos were of the Priory and the Watch House at the mouth of the Tyne.

On my early travels around Britain, long before I picked up a camera with any serious intention, the seaside looms large in my memory. Holidays with my grandmother at Butlins, Filey (coincidentally, while shooting this book I lived a mile from the Butlins site), and further out to Torquay and Paignton; day trips to Skegness, Berwick and Bamburgh. During a brief sojourn in the West Country I ended up on the cob at Lyme Regis and on Clevedon Pier. When others' travels in Britain simply involved getting to and from an airport, I would prefer to be in Cornwall or on the west coast of Scotland. And so I found my way to the Yorkshire Coast. I think it was a natural progression; perhaps I was intended to be here.

In the course of working on this project for over two years, I have seen much of what this coastline has to offer. The sun has risen and set, sometimes baking the shores, sometimes being blotted out by snow clouds. Storms have ravaged the cliffs and children have paddled in calm water. Huge coastal features have collapsed and been washed away to be deposited as new coastal features elsewhere. People have died – I am often reminded of that by flowers laid at cliff edges – and people have been saved by the brave work of the volunteer lifeboatmen, coastguards and the Royal Navy.

This book is not about the people or societies of the coastline, and I make no apology for that. They belong in books by other photographers;

I am no Frank Meadow Sutcliffe. Indeed, I try to make people invisible or peripheral characters in my work, although inevitably the human hand will have had a bearing on most of the scenes I am shooting. Neither is this a history book or an accurate textual record of how the coast has developed. It is about the landscape itself, a visual record of how processes that remain beyond our control have shaped it into its current form and relentlessly continue to change it. Primarily it is intended to be looked at, not read. If someone looked at every photograph, but didn't read a single word, I would be delighted.

If there is any underlying theme to this work, it's only that we should enjoy and care for the coast while it lasts (assuming it is possible to simultaneously 'enjoy' and 'care' for the coast). It won't be there for ever, at least not in its current form. I am tempted to say it won't be there for much longer. The threat of global warming looms larger every day. Current scientific knowledge suggests two main possibilities for our climate in the British Isles. In the first scenario, the steady rise in global temperature will lead to the melting of the polar ice caps and Greenland. The trapped water in Greenland alone has the potential to raise our sea levels by 7 metres. Rising seas will inundate low-lying areas of the Yorkshire Coast, such as Whitby Harbour and the Scarborough foreshore with frightening regularity, not to mention decimating the flat sandbanks of Spurn and threatening the entire city of Hull. Higher tides will also speed the erosion of weak areas such as the Holderness Coast and Filey Brigg.

The second scenario is even harder to contemplate, in that the polar melting and increased rainfall produced by global warming could weaken or even stop the Gulf Stream, the global conveyor of heat that benefits the UK so much. Our climate could rapidly begin to match that of areas at similar latitudes, such as Alaska and parts of Siberia. The coastline could be extended by miles of sea ice during long, bleak winters.

Nothing is certain, though few climate scientists envisage things continuing as they are. Regardless of who or what is to blame, that is just not the way the planet tends to operate. So enjoy the Yorkshire coast while it lasts.

'There is something about the light in Staithes that is completely timeless. When the sun etches out the lines of the houses, dawn becomes indistinguishable from dusk. It is a place that is on the verge of something terrible about to happen, a village so close to the sea that one always gets the impression that the sea itself wants to claw it back beneath the waves. Perhaps Staithes was bought at a price, cut from the cliff and fortified against the weather by stone walls and barricades. The village clings to the rocks like limpets to a boulder as the tide washes in. It is easy to imagine some terrible force of water blasting its way down from the high moor and washing every stone into the sea in anger at the arrogance of man to dare to live at the edge of the land. Some years ago I took the Lifeboat Day service and our singing was drowned out by the call of the gulls. As I stood to preach I shouted "Peace be still!" On cue, the birds that circled above our heads were silenced. One old fisherman came up later in the pub and said "Don't worry Vicar. Weren't nothing supernatural. Once they find the roost they all go silent." Silent Staithes, just after dawn: waiting, foreboding, fragile and wonderful.' G.P.T.

previous pages
A short uphill walk from Staithes village leads to Cowbar Nab. Here a comprehensive panorama springs into view – the village encircled by the curving Staithes Beck. The Yorkshire coast begins in fine style.

above
The classic view of Staithes and one of the iconic scenes of the Yorkshire coast. From here it is easy to imagine that the village has changed little in over a century.

right
Slate grey skies tinged with evening colour match the slates of the terraced cottages and remind me of my first visit to Staithes, back in 1990. The village takes on a brooding persona with threatening skies – very different to its chocolate-box image.

Flowering gorse, seen here at Port Mulgrave, is a classic sign of spring, although the species seems easily confused by our warmer winters. A mild spell in December or January can bring an unexpected dash of colour.

A mile or so down the coast from Staithes is Old Nab. The cliffs to the east and west of Staithes are not easily accessible, though some areas can be visited after carefully checking the tide tables. The majority of the land bordering the coast is agricultural, an extreme example of which is here at Old Nab, where sheep graze within yards of the cliff edge.

A day of drama on the coast at Runswick; looking out towards Kettleness, a rainbow dips below heaped stormcloud.

The relaxed village of Runswick Bay lies five miles to the south-east of Staithes, but stands in contrast to its more famous neighbour. Again, Cornwall is strongly evoked, but this time by the tranquil whitewashed cottages rather than by the rugged, workmanlike beauty of Staithes. Runswick is set at the head of an expansive bay that runs two miles south-west to Kettleness, and is one of the lesser-known gems of the Yorkshire coast.

18

previous pages
The groynes at the outflow
of Sandsend Beck always
offer great inspiration for
photographers. Like Staithes
and Whitby, Sandsend may
appear to have originated as
a fishing port, but it actually
began life as a major alum
works, the entire village
being dedicated to its
production. Now there is
little to distinguish it from
any other bustling resort.

The Yorkshire coast provides many days
of inclement weather, but few are so
photogenic. Sweeping stormclouds and
flickering sunlight provide some of the
most inspirational conditions I have yet
seen on this coast.

right
Whitby harbour from the clifftop graveyard of St Mary the Virgin. The coast here runs from west to east, and in summer the sun sets well to the north, throwing light on to the bays and beaches. On this occasion a powerful thunderstorm was making its way out to sea to the right of frame, a few hours after causing flash-floods in Helmsley.

below
One of the classic perspectives of Whitby Abbey – looking west across the Abbey pond and into a summer afterglow.

'For many years a story circulated that the ghost of St Hilda walked the high ramparts of the ruined abbey. Later it was revealed to be a trick of the light, the setting sun casting a shadow into one of the high windows. Humankind always wants to plant its stone feet on the earth to rival God and all creation. As we stare and are captivated by the blues of the sky and the black earth, how feeble our own creations seem in comparison. The best that we can do is to build in stone and mortar and, like our feeble bodies, watch them decay and return to dust while all around is that which is eternal and renewed every morning.' G.P.T.

Walkers take in the sea
air on a relaxed summer
evening in Whitby.

Just one of the classic views of Whitby, looking east towards St Mary the Virgin
on a hot summer day. Children play at the waters edge on a muddy beach formed
by the sea walls and tourists gather in the pub gardens and on the clifftops.

Built in the tenth century and largely destroyed by Henry VIII's Reformation, Whitby Abbey remains the architectural icon of the Yorkshire coast. It now resembles the disintegrating ribcage of a giant dinosaur that came to rest on the clifftop. Catching the abbey in good light is not too hard, given its position. A full moon in January competes with a foreboding sky whilst late sunshine illuminates the remaining stones.

A spectacular sunset surrounding
Whitby Abbey captured after a
December afternoon at Saltwick Bay.

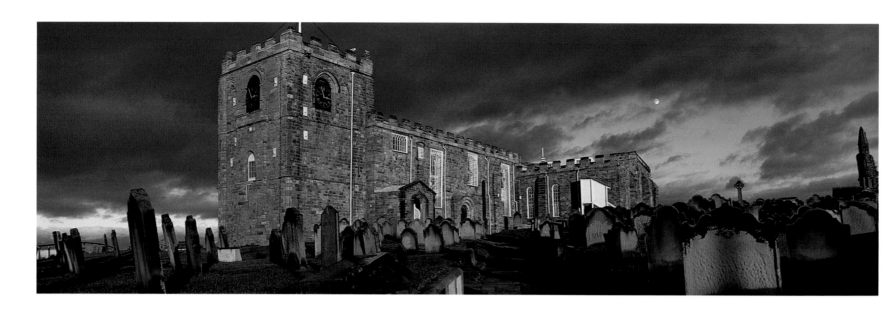

'Everyone has a special place that they return to time and time again in their life. For thousands of people the church of St Mary the Virgin has an almost hypnotic quality as a place of pilgrimage. If you stand in the church porch at midnight on Hallowe'en you will be visited by vampires coming to celebrate the first bite that Dracula took out of Mina's neck by a gravestone not far away. Witches return each year to renew their wedding vows on the clifftop and Christians from around the world visit the site in countless numbers each year. There is something about its stones that give out the presence of a creator. Regardless of creed it can touch all of our lives. It has been a backdrop for Hollywood movies and pop videos, the place of happiness and great sadness. The graves that surround the church tell the story of the growth of the town they overlook. Fishermen and paupers nestle next to the rich and infamous.' G.P.T.

A hive of activity for centuries, Whitby harbour still bustles with activity. Pleasure craft are now more numerous than its proud fishing fleet.

St Mary the Virgin – the church immortalised in Bram
Stoker's *Dracula* – looking suitably gothic in evening sunshine.
The earliest parts of the building date from 1110 and, despite
some obvious subsidence, it has thankfully survived intact.

Whitby's harbour is defended by twin curving piers
complemented by weathered sandstone lighthouses. Here
'earth shadow' – the reflection of the earth's surface after
sunset – provides a contrasting backdrop to one of the
towers, while Saltwick Nab is visible in silhouette to the right
of frame.

Late rays of January sunshine hit Saltwick Nab, while light rebounds from polished Whitby jet in the cliff.

Looking north-west at the midsummer sunset, the light catches on the reflective shales of Saltwick Bay.

Saltwick Nab photographed from the part of the cliff it once belonged to, with winter sunlight striking the whale's tail and the North Sea looking bluer than blue.

Saltwick Nab may appear entirely natural, but has actually been shaped more by man than by the waves, cut from the surrounding cliff by the once dominant alum industry. Inadvertently, the distinctive whale-shaped outcrop emerged, complete with a 'tail-fin' smaller stack.

The remains of a fishing boat that ended its days behind Black Nab must be one of Britain's most photographed shipwrecks. Only parts of the hull and engine block remain now and, like the natural features of the coastline, it won't be there for ever. However, the sea is always capable of claiming new victims.

Low tide in midsummer is a favourite time to shoot at Saltwick, with large areas of flat shale and still pools of water to reflect the setting sun. It is increasingly popular amongst photographers and this image was taken alongside Joe Cornish and a dozen members of York Camera Club. The spacious wave-cut platform means that there's usually enough room for everyone!

Skies and their reflections change colour rapidly as the sun approaches the horizon. Like Saltwick Nab itself, Black Nab was carved out of the surrounding cliff by alum hunters rather than by tidal action. This stack of harder rock escaped their attention and stands defiant against the turbulent seas.

'Who would believe that hundreds of ships once crowded into this peaceful place? Hundreds of people gathered upon the rocks to pick jet, sea coal and alum. Donkeys and carts bustled along at low tide and the smoke of fires filled the air with caustic fumes that swirled in the heat of the shouts and squabbles that rumpused from the ragged upon the shore. Smugglers hid contraband, lovers found their first kiss and wondered of the strange footprints cut into the bedrock. What would it be like if the stones could recount all they have seen and heard: the echoing cries of the Rohilla as it sank to the depths and the laughter of children as they picked whelks? Stand here, look upon these stones and feel the earth beneath your feet. Tread carefully for fear of the hag worms and know that one day soon your bones will be as dry and brittle as the alum. You will see this place no more, yet it will still be here for other eyes to see and dream the dreams that are now in your head.' G.P.T.

SMUGGLER'S COAST

previous pages
The distinctive headland of Ravenscar,
as seen from Robin Hood's Bay on a
winter afternoon.

below
Sledgates Hill above Robin Hood's Bay
provides a fine vantage point from
which to view the village and the sea.
Reaching the brow of the hill before
plunging down the gradient towards
Fylingthorpe is a memorable
experience, and a good test for brakes.

White fluffy clouds drift across
Robin Hood's Bay on a picture-
perfect afternoon in late summer.

right
Captured in afternoon sunlight, Robin Hood's Bay displays all the characteristics that make it one of the most popular tourist destinations on the Yorkshire coast.

below
May Day; and after a wedding at the Raven Hall Hotel, the evening skies come together in celebration over Robin Hood's Bay.

'There is a legend that Bram Stoker, on his famous trip to Whitby, took a train to Ravenscar, alighted at the hotel and walked along the battlements. They say it was here that he got his inspiration for the land of Transylvania and the battle with the vampire in Dracula's castle. As the sun sets over the sea it reminds us more of the warmth of the south. The land is placated by the heavens, the sea is calm and all is well with the world. From the battlements we can dream magenta dreams as our minds take us far away.' G.P.T.

'How many of us have dreamed of finding a precious jewel at the bottom of a rock pool? Age takes away our dreams and our play. What was once another world in which to immerse ourselves becomes a clumsy obstacle to our boot-clad walk across the rocks in Robin Hood's Bay. What once would fascinate becomes a dreary part of the picture our dimming eyes glance upon. Captured here is the perfect dream of childhood: a fresh pool on a deserted shore that we will share with no one. We will search for fish and chew upon the seaweed as we dip our feet in the cool water and lick the salt from our lips, imagine the sand to be a desert and the pool to be the edge of a great sea. Search for what you lost when childhood ended, where the sun on the water and the shadow of a cloud becomes the wing of an angel captured from the corner of an eye.' G.P.T.

Midway between Robin Hood's Bay and Ravenscar lies Boggle Hole, a sea cut formed by Ramsdale Beck on its way to the sea. Water also flows from the boulder clay cliffs after wet weather, and cascades on to the beach in a number of waterfalls, saturating the beach at low tide.

Melancholy evening light bounces from one of the many tidal pools on Robin Hood Bay's.

Dry coastal grasses blow in a freshening wind, signalling the end of a fruitful summer at Ravenscar.

'Peak offers its cheek to the volatile North Sea. The road from the south once followed the beach and up the landing into Robin Hood's Bay. Now storms eat the cliff and pull acre after acre to the sea. It is here that the high moor plunges 600 feet and the gouges of the old alum works are slowly reclaimed by the wilderness with every passing year. This gigantic cove is the place of many legends and myths, dreamed by the hundreds of people who once lived here. High up on the cliff the old Peak House dominates the landscape, a place once lost in a bet over two woodlice running across a plate. From the strand it appears as a cragged outcrop of dark stone. The whole feels as if it were part of a Jurassic landscape. What was once fought over by smugglers and rogues is now in the hands of the preservation men, and locals quarrel over every brick and sill they wish to lay.' G.P.T.

Midway between Robin Hood's Bay and Scarborough lies Hayburn Wyke, where twin waterfalls from Hayburn Beck pour on to a small rocky beach.

'The waterfall at Hayburn Beck is a place of power, majesty and might. The water deafens your ears and pounds the stones to shingle. The shore is littered with driftwood, always too soaked to burn but still many try. It is a place of midnight parties and ghost stories told beneath a full moon. It always remains the same and is best seen in winter as the water rushes through the woods towards the sea and the chill breeze from the north cuts against the skin. I often wonder who was the first ever person to look upon this place. What eyes first glanced over the rocks?' G.P.T.

46

'Scarborough Castle has been a force in so many people's lives: a Royalist stronghold that stood against the might of Cromwell, a prison for Fox, the founder of the Quaker movement and, for many, a place of childhood dreams. From the north and from the south it gives the impression of Camelot – and yet in history it never saw much of any king. Castles always leave me with a feeling of dread, as if the stones speak out, calling to us all of what has gone on within.' G.P.T.

previous pages
Colours gather on Scalby Ness as the gorse flowers on the earth banks in late spring. Although the nab is protected by a lower layer of solid rock, the soft boulder clay on top still erodes with the wind, rain and high seas.

right
The setting sun in December brings red tones to the sandstone blocks of Scarborough Castle, while cumulus clouds gather out to sea.

below
Sunlight glints from the hotels and flats of North Bay, on a snowy December afternoon in Scarborough.

Sea mist rolls in and ends what had previously been a winter's day of bright sunlight. The view from the castle walls faces Oliver's Mount, reputedly named after Oliver Cromwell. His Parliamentarian forces besieged the castle in 1644, and the hill was used as a vantage point for the army.

Almost exactly two years later, snow coats rooftops across Scarborough. The two scenes, shot from the same path below the castle walls, represent the beginning and the end of my two-year project to record the Yorkshire Coast on film.

'When I was a child I stood on the ridge between the sea and Scalby Beck and wondered how this finger of land came to exist. If you enquire closely behind the grass and sedge you will see the hand of man. This was once the place of an isolation hospital and an army machine gun range. How different now! How Nature reclaims all our calamities!' G.P.T.

50

Scarborough is the entertainment capital of the Yorkshire coast, with its amusement arcades and chip shops attracting trade even in the colder months. The image of Las Vegas on the Yorkshire coast is perhaps not to all residents' taste but the opening of a multi-million pound casino in 2005 brings it a little closer to reality, if on a small scale.

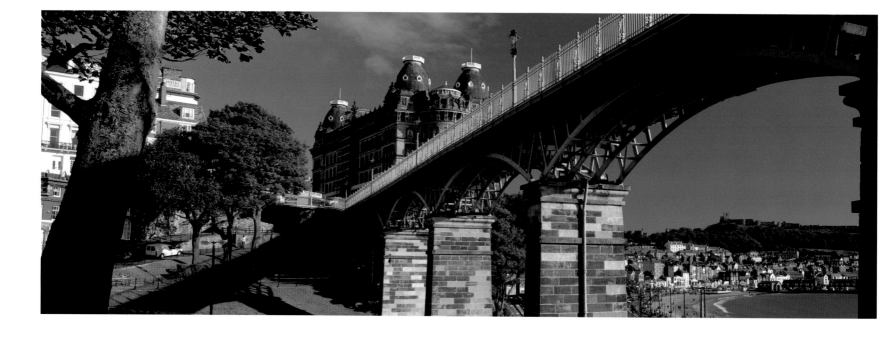

The fishing industry still exists in Scarborough, but times have certainly changed since its heyday. Now the rugged hulks of working boats are heavily outnumbered by yachts.

Underneath the elegant Spa Bridge on Scarborough's South
Bay, a view that has changed very little since Victorian times.
Built in 1827, Spa Bridge predates the height of Scarborough's
importance as a tourist destination, although its Georgian
grandeur will have helped in first attracting visitors.

above

Melting frost makes for treacherous conditions on the
Spa Bridge, but the Grand looks at its finest in the crisp
winter light.

left

The windows of the Grand on the south side of the
building command spectacular views down the
Yorkshire coast. In 140 years the residents will have
witnessed some tremendous skies. When completed in
1867 the Grand Hotel was one of the largest hotels in
the world and its rooms hosted the wealthy and famous.
Although times have moved on, a return to such glory
days is never out of the question.

*'The Grand has a window for every day of the year, a turret
for each season and a floor for every month. All in all, it is a
gigantic clock. Hitler said that if he were to conquer Britain
then he would have summer home in the Grand Hotel. It is a
building that takes time to appreciate – stand back and look,
admire each brick and cornice, look at the faces of the statues
and listen to the music from another age.' G.P.T.*

Blues from a darkening September sky are reflected
in tidal pools on Scarborough's South Bay.

Gently lapping seas give little indication of furious waves that were to follow later the same day. Only mounting cloud on the horizon offers any clue to the changing conditions.

'These images show us the battle between land and sea, earth and sky. The calm before the storm, time to retreat to our shelters, barricade the door and sit about the fire.' G.P.T.

Destructive waves crash into Scarborough's sea defences. Similar spring tides in 1993 led to a large slump in the boulder clay above this point. The ensuing collapse of the Holbeck Hall Hotel was seen on television all around the world, and, curiously, is likely to remain one of the most famous events in Scarborough's long history. Here I am standing on the reinforced landslip, and no doubt on debris from the hotel itself, in danger of getting very wet.

The view of Scarborough from Oliver's Mount is one of
the best known on the Yorkshire coast. On this January
afternoon the thick layer of cloud looked set to prevent
any opportunity for photography, but just before sunset
a small break appeared and the town was illuminated by
a brief spell of golden light.

Tidal water next to the sea wall mirrors the imposing Grand Hotel on a bright December afternoon.

The venerable Spa Theatre under a threatening winter sky.
With some views of Scarborough it is easy to imagine
oneself to be on a day trip to the age of Victoria.

A dog-walker on Scarborough's
South Bay adds a sense of scale to
the view that runs all the way to
Flamborough Head.

Minutes after dawn in December, Filey Brigg reveals colours comparable to the Arizona wilderness or Ayers Rock.

A large tidal pool reflects the evening sky on the seaweed-clad shore around Filey Brigg.

In late-December sunlight, walkers fade into the surroundings next to Filey Brigg. Although underpinned by a foundation of solid rock, high tides and rain water continually wear away at the boulder clay upper layer of Filey Brigg. This causes frequent slumps on to the beach, a similar process to the constant erosion of the Holderness coastline further south. Sections of Carr Naze are continually becoming more dangerous for walkers to traverse. Within a lifetime the earthen banks could be a memory, leaving only the rocky lower layers of Filey Brigg that protrude into the North Sea.

'This was once the playground of J.R.R. Tolkein. One summer when he was here, his son lost a metal dog on the beach. This event provided the start of his novellette "Roverandom". Filey is the second cousin once removed of its neighbour to the north, a genteel place and truly a forgotten jewel. I prefer Filey to Cannes any day. It has a life and vitality that cannot be taken away. The sky really is this colour and the lights do dance like jewels on velvet.' G.P.T.

A fiery dawn adds warmth to a frozen morning on Filey Bay. When skies are clear, winter often provides greater opportunities for photography as the cold air and prevailing winds give the atmosphere greater clarity.

The beach just to the south of Filey Brigg often remains saturated well after the tide has fallen, creating a mirror-like surface. This is ideal for reflecting evening colours and cloud.

'A birdless sky as the sun sets. No gannets or guillemots, not even a common gull to squawk above our heads. Chalk rises form a still sea as the sun is consumed beneath the Oceanus Germanicus. Is is said that to find Asgard all you had to do was walk the sunlit path across the waves. He who can walk on water can lead us to Heaven. How great the ocean is, and how mighty its power! Staring at the sunset from the clifftop gives you the feeling of being so minute, so tiny in a vast universe. The brightness of the sun grows with each second and just before it finally vanishes we are given the delight of a piercing diamond.' G.P.T.

Late February, and storms sweep in from the North Sea over Filey Bay making for a dramatic end to the day. Conditions such as these can be frustrating and unpleasant for the photographer, but the rewards are greater if the clouds break apart.

The day after a heavy snowfall in January, rivers of meltwater stream from the cliffs across Reighton Sands, catching the reflection of the azure sky.

following pages
Low tide and high summer is an ideal combination for shooting on the Yorkshire coast. In late May, the last rays of sun are beginning to find the outer ridges of sand at Hunmanby Gap. The variety in colour, texture, light and shadow is remarkable on such an apparently blank canvas.

Yorkshire beaches represented ideal targets for landing during a possible German invasion in World War II. The evidence of this is still visible at many places along the coastline, most notably at Spurn and near the mouth of the Humber, but also at Flamborough and here on Filey Bay. Now waves and weather are reducing these buildings to their constituent elements, and soon there will be little to distinguish many of them from rocks and pebbles on the beaches.

Violet 'earth shadow' in late spring gives a
haunting appearance to Bempton Cliffs.

previous pages, right and below
Low tide at Thornwick Nab on the northern coast of Flamborough. The midsummer sun dips into the North Sea, casting magnificent light on the lingering cloud and contrails. There are no better views of Bempton Cliffs from land than at this point, accessible for only a few hours each day at low tide.

Emerging from a tiny gap between the cloud base and land, the setting sun casts a beam of light across the waters of Filey Bay. A posy of flowers at my feet served as a reminder to approach the edge with extreme caution. No year passes without a death, accidental or otherwise, on the Yorkshire coast cliffs.

'We think we are the master of our planet. For me, the sea is the master, as it has life and death within its power. It plays with us, cajoles us and tempts us, invites us to sail on it, then crashes on to the decks and engulfs all our efforts. The waves will crash and pound the rocks grinding them to sand. We build our barricades but the patience of the sea will always overcome. Gone will be the passion of men to stem the tide. Sand and sea will take from us all we own.' G.P.T.

A rainstorm passes Flamborough Head in mid-June. The enormity of the sea always captivates me, and I am often inspired to turn my camera to face it, removing all traces of land and emphasising its power.

A gnarled outcrop of rock protrudes at low tide
in Thornwick Bay. Small pebbles are trapped in
cavities in the limestone and gradually grind
away with the tides, riddling the tidal shelves
with circular holes. This forms a contrast to the
polished chalk surfaces further up the beach,
near the high-water line.

Standing on top of cliffs that eroded many years ago, looking back to those that stand today. The final layer of topsoil forms curious conical piles as is erodes, caused more by the rain than by heavy seas.

After sunset Thornwick Cliffs appear to fluoresce with light captured earlier in the day.

Early March, and the sun is already setting far enough to the north to cast light on the Thornwick Cliffs. In the foreground, tidal wash creates whirlpools and streaks on the rocks. I am always mesmerised by such movement.

Dark storm clouds pass across Thornwick Cliffs. I sheltered from the squalls under a rocky overhang next to Thornwick Nab, taking my opportunites for shots when the showers subsided.

A wonderful location at dawn, or here at high summer, the white cliffs of Thornwick Bay catch any remaining glance from the sun and reflect the rays back into the cove.

When I first stood on a precipitous outcrop above Thornwick Bay and spotted the Major Arch, I felt that I had found the definitive view of the coast, or at least the definitive view of the 'wild' side of the Yorkshire shores. Unlike much of this coastline, human intervention has done little to affect this particular scene. Although light was fading fast, I was still compelled to make one attempt to photograph the view. After almost ten minutes of continuous exposure I decided that enough light would have fallen on the film to make the shot at least viewable. On seeing the result, I was surprised to find that it was still chronically underexposed, but that this underexposure had worked wonders bringing out the deep blues of the sea and contrasting the elegant archway in ethereal cold light. A year after I had first photographed the Major Arch, and around nine months after my most recent visit, I returned to the spot with two eager friends to rediscover the view. Initially my instincts told me that we were in the wrong place, or not far enough out on the outcrop. However, the cliff edge was just yards away, and the foreground familiar. The Major Arch was gone, just like so many forgotten coastal features before it. The view was unrecognisable. In the days afterwards I tried to find out what had become of the arch. As the plinth where it stood was so clean and flat, as if sliced by cheese wire, I thought that perhaps this had been a controlled demolition by safety experts. On speaking to East Riding Council, I discovered this was not the case. The arch must have collapsed by natural means in late 2004 or early 2005 and any residue quickly dispersed by the tides. My back catalogue of slides revealed a substantial vertical crack in the stone. The archway had been on borrowed time. I suspect only seabirds were present to witness its departure.

A sea gorge on the eastern rim of Thornwick Bay. Such features are usually formed when the roof of a large cave collapses. Fifty yards away another great sea cave awaits this next stage of its development.

Incoming tides create a remarkable whirlpool feature beside Flamborough's sadly departed Major Arch.

North Landing, an enclosed cove to the east of
Thornwick, has enough protection from the
elements to harbour a fleet of small fishing boats.
On this July evening the North Sea was in as benign
a mood as possible, and puffins skimmed gracefully
across the still green water.

Pounding spring tides engulf the
ageing concrete slipway at North
Landing, Flamborough.

Fishing boats sit angled on the
slipway, dragged to safety by an
impossibly corroded yet still
active tractor.

Selwick is the most easterly of Flamborough's four main bays. Rocks at the fringes of the high tides are polished like glass, while above they are coarse and stained by impurities and algae. Sea birds perch on what is surprisingly Flamborough's only accessible sea stack. Such stacks remain when sea caves form archways, which in turn collapse. Flamborough Head, like much of the Yorkshire coastline, is continually eroding, but it is doing so far more slowly, as can be seen simply by looking at the map. It protrudes from the line formed by Holderness and the North Yorkshire coast by around ten miles, and this will only increase as the centuries go by.

Dating from 1806, the second lighthouse built at Flamborough still powers a beam of light across the North Sea to warn shipping of the dangers posed by the peninsula. The last resident lighthouse keeper left in 1996, but it is still in pristine condition thanks to maintenance by Trinity House.

Gathering shadows signal another night of
active service for Flamborough Lighthouse.

While lacking some of the intricate coastal features of the other bays at Flamborough, South Landing is still a superb location to catch the dawn or dusk in winter. Here, the sun sets over the town of Bridlington.

The incoming tide rolls across the chalk boulders of South Landing beach.

'I remember the day when, three miles out to sea, we found that someone had drilled several holes in the bottom of my uncle's Flamborough cobble. It was one of those moments where a life at sea told him what to do. He showed no emotion as the deck boards began to ooze water and the boat slowly sank. The sabotage was working and it looked as if we wouldn't make it back to South Landing. Bravely he turned to the south and the far away lights of Bridlington Harbour. Closer and closer the cobble bobbed in the waves, its bows sinking lower as it took on more water. He never doubted that he would make it. A steely grin on his face, he mused deep within on who it was who would do such a deed. As the cobble limped into the harbour, the benches were filled with tourists – all oblivious to what could have taken place. It was slack water and the boat was beached on the mud. I have never been so thankful for the sight of Bridlington. I would later come back to watch David Bowie, Thin Lizzy and every other band who played the spa. It would become a second home of friendship and love and late-night walks to the end of the pier to remember times past when we all almost became an offering to the sea.'
G.P.T.

previous pages
The rising sun illuminates Bridlington sea front
in a riot of colour.

left and below
Scuttling cloud hurries past Bridlington Pier,
on a cold December morning.

An abandoned ring of sandcastles await the tide after a summer's day at Hornsea. The town's tourist beach is defended by an extensive network of groynes. The tall sea wall defends the town itself, and the promenade is beginning to jut out from the undefended coastline on either side of the town.

While Bridlington has much better natural defences against erosion than the Holderness coast, groynes were still erected to prevent the popular tourist beaches shifting south.

left and following pages
A post marking the end of a lengthy groyne gives a sense of scale to intricate summer cloud formations near the Holderness Coast town of Hornsea.

Remnants of fishing nets litter Spurn Point and cling to the survivors of the extensive system of groynes on the eastern beach. Current wisdom would not allow money to be wasted on building such sea defences; they provided only a delay to the erosion process and can exacerbate problems elsewhere. The deserted lighthouse at Spurn will be one day be claimed by the sea. The entire sand bar is shifting to the west, and the road to the coastguard station at the southerly tip is under constant threat. In March 2005 parts were destroyed by heavy seas and have now been replaced with portable rubber sections that can be moved and reinstalled.

A passing raincloud gives water back to the sea off the coast at Mappleton, Holderness. The grassy ridge in the foreground represents another new frontier on one of the world's fastest eroding coastlines, and will soon be removed by heavy seas or wet weather.

The upright posts of the decaying groynes at Spurn Point now stand like sculptures, as if to commemorate man's failed attempts to control the elements.

TECHNICALITIES

After experimenting with a number of 35mm and medium-format cameras, I was continually dreaming of larger and larger formats to give extra detail on the slide and hence better quality. Inspired by the work of Joe Cornish, a 5 x 4 inch view camera might have been an obvious choice, but I didn't want to go down that route for a number of reasons. The first was my complete inexperience of using such a camera and single sheet film. Swing and tilt – the 'movements' of view cameras were at the time alien concepts to me and I felt that it would have taken me too long to grasp them, given that I still had much to learn about exposure and composition. Another consideration was the cost of setting up such a system with a choice of lenses, and film, which could cost around £5 per photo to shoot and process. Failed exposures would be costly and there were bound to be many of them. Finally, and most importantly, I didn't want to be seen attempting to copy Joe's work, however badly. It was likely that I would be visiting a number of similar locations, and I wanted a distinctive format, something a little different to the standard 3 x 2 ratio of 35mm and square 'Hasselblad' 6 x 6cm format.

I'd owned a copy of Colin Prior's *Scotland – The Wild Places* for a while, when it became a fixture on our coffee table in early 2003, despite my wife's best efforts to tidy it away. I had finally settled on a camera and a very distinctive format – panoramic. While marvelling at the unspoilt beauty of Colin's landscapes, I had also been studying the detail and technical aspects of his photographs. The 6 x 17cm format is so pleasing to my eye. Perhaps it is because it is necessary to pan across it with the eyes to pick out detail, in much the same way you would with a real landscape. Conversely, perhaps it is because the eyes take it all in; after all, we generally see in 'panoramic' format. Whichever is the case, half the battle was over; I had made my choice.

A few months later, after much saving of precious funds, I invested in my first 617 format camera, the Fuji G617. First manufactured in 1985, it employs a 105mm Fujinon fixed lens of superb quality, covering 83 degrees of the landscape. The width of the lens coverage means that light finds it harder to reach the edges of the frame than the centre, so a 'centre filter' with a darkened centre spot is required to correct this. This usually stays on the camera at all times. A great advantage is that the 617 format takes standard 120 roll film, on which you take four images per roll, bringing the cost per shot down to around £1.50. To be precise, the transparencies measure 56 x 168mm, giving an area 10.88 times the size of 35mm film and consequently high quality. The deluxe version, the GX617, released by Fuji some years later, had the advantage of four interchangeable lenses at 90, 105, 180 and 300mm. Sadly Fuji discontinued the GX617 in the first half of 2005 as they moved away from their professional film camera range to concentrate entirely on digital capture. My first successful shots with the G617 were in July 2003 and later in the year I started on the project that would eventually become this book.

Later, I was offered the opportunity to use a new camera in the same format, made by a small Hong Kong outfit called Fotoman. The Fotoman 617 has the advantage of being adaptable for use with a large variety of large format lenses, such as Schnieder, Rodenstock and even Fuji. A small number of images from this book were shot with this camera. With this set-up I am using a 90mm Caltar lens and a 180mm Rodenstock. Fotoman provide a variety of 'cones', which adapt the lenses to be used with the same camera body. While I have not used it as much as a Fuji, it appears to be a very useful system, and I shall be testing it more fully.

The question many ask is 'Why film?' as if this is a retrograde method for photography. Some people are very surprised when they find that all my panoramas are shot this way. There are a number of reasons.

The first is the film itself. For most of my work I use Fuji Velvia 50asa. The colour saturation and 'look' of Velvia is what I want from my photography. Perhaps in certain circumstances the saturation level of this film is too much, but generally I think it produces colours that do the landscape justice and are realistic. Digital often looks dull by comparison and any attempt to enhance the colour in software packages tends to make things look unnatural. I have also found using film for long exposures preferable to digital, particularly when dealing with moving water, one of my favourite subjects.

The second reason is detail. Although high-end digital cameras achieving around 16 megapixels are now arguably matching medium format cameras, to shoot panoramically with similar detail to film would require 'stitching' separate images together, which often leads to problems with perspective.

To control the exposure on my Velvia I employ two highly accurate light meters, the Pentax Digital Spotmeter and Gossen Spotmaster. Balancing light and shadow is a must with a film as sensitive as Velvia. To do this I use the Lee resin filter system, using their neutral density graduated filters to reduce the brightness of skies. These superb filters make no alterations to colour in the image; they are used to return the balance of light to what the human eye sees. Film is far less adaptable than the eye and needs help to capture all the detail of a particular scene. I also occasionally use Lee warm-up filters to return warmer tones to the film when shooting in full shadow or without sunlight and a Lee polarizer to enhance blue skies and reduce glare in bright conditions.

With exposures rarely lasting less than a quarter of a second, a good camera support is essential, and for this book I have used Manfrotto and Benbo tripods.

PHOTOGRAPHIC INFORMATION

page 1
2s at f22, 0.6 ND grad.
January 2005

pages 2–3
1s at f22, 0.9 ND grad.
December 2005

pages 4–5
1s at f32, unfiltered.
May 2005

page 7
1/15s at f8, polarizer.
December 2004

pages 8–9
8s at f22, 81c.
April 2005

pages 10–11
1s at f22, 0.6 ND grad.
November 2004

pages 10–11
5s at f22, 0.6 ND grad.
February 2005

page 12
1/4s at f22, 0.3 ND grad.
February 2005

page 13
1/4s at f22, 0.6 ND grad.
February 2005

page 14
1s at f22, 0.3 ND grad, polarizer.
February 2005

page 15
1s at f22, 0.9 ND grad.
November 2005

pages 16–17
12s at f22, 0.6 ND grad.
April 2005

page 18
1/2s at f16, 0.6 ND grad.
November 2005

page 19
1s at f16, 0.9 ND grad.
November 2005

All photographs were taken with a Fuji G617 Professional Film Camera, (105mm Fujinon lens) with Fuji Velvia 50asa film, unless stated, and used a Fuji 0.3 ND centre filter. All other filters referred to are Lee. ND = Neutral density; grad = graduated.

pages 20–21
5s at f16, 0.6 ND grad.
June 2005

pages 20–1
12s at f16, 0.6 ND grad.
June 2005

pages 22–3
1s at f22, 0.3 ND grad, polarizer.
August 2005

page 23
1/2s at f16, 0.6 ND grad, polarizer.
July 2005

pages 24–5
1s at f16, 0.6 ND grad.
January 2005

pages 24–5
2s at f22, 0.6 ND.
December 2003

page 26
1/15s at f11, 0.6 ND grad.
January 2005

page 26
5s at f22, unfiltered.
May 2004

page 27
1/2s at f22, 0.6 ND grad.
December 2003

pages 28–9
25s at f32, 0.9 ND grad.
June 2004

pages 28–9
12s at f32, 0.9 ND grad (on side), 0.6 ND grad.
November 2004

pages 30–31
1s at f22, 0.6 ND grad.
February 2004

page 31
1s at f22, 0.6 ND grad.
November 2003

page 32
8s at f22, 0.6 ND grad.
June 2005

page 33
12s at f22, 0.6 ND grad, 81ef.
May 2004

page 33
4s at f22, 0.6 ND grad.
June 2005

pages 34–5
½s at f22, 0.3 ND grad.
November 2004

pages 36–7
1s at f22, 0.6 ND grad, polarizer.
September 2005

page 37
1s at f22, 0.6 ND grad, polarizer.
September 2005

pages 38–9
1s at f32, 0.6 ND grad.
November 2004

pages 38–9
10s at f22, 0.6 ND grad.
May 2004

pages 40–1
6s at f22, 0.9 ND grad.
December 2005

page 41
30s at f32, unfiltered.
November 2004

page 42
5s at f32, 0.9 ND grad, polarizer.
September 2005

page 43
1m at f16, 81ef.
April 2004

pages 44–5
3s at f22, 0.9 ND grad.
April 2005

pages 46–7
1s at f16, 0.6 ND grad.
December 2005

page 47
4s at f22, 0.6 ND grad, polarizer.
December 2003

pages 48–9
1s at f16, 0.9 ND grad.
December 2003

page 48
2s at f16, 0.9 ND grad.
December 2005

page 50
1/4s at f22, 0.3 ND grad.
September 2004

page 51
2m at f16, unfiltered.
October 2004

page 51
15s at f32, 0.9 ND grad.
December 2004

pages 52–3
1s at f22, 0.6 ND grad, polarizer.
November 2004

pages 52
1/4s at f16, polarizer.
October 2004

pages 54–5
1s at f22, 0.6 ND grad.
September 2004

page 56
1/2s at f22, 0.6 ND grad, polarizer.
March 2005

page 56
1/30s at f8, 0.6 ND grad, pushed 1 stop.
March 2005

page 57
1/30s at f8, 0.6 ND
grad, pushed 1 stop.
Mar 2005

pages 58–9
1s at f22, 0.6 ND grad.
December 2003

pages 60–1
12s at f22, 0.9 ND grad, 0.6 ND grad (staggered).
December 2003

pages 60–1
1s at f22, 0.3 ND grad.
January 2004

pages 62–3
1/2s at f22, 0.6 ND grad.
October 2004

pages 64–5
4s at f22, 0.6 ND grad, polarizer.
December 2005

124

page 66
8s at f22, 0.6 ND grad.
December 2003

page 66
5s at f32, 0.9 ND grad.
December 2005

page 67
5s at f22, 0.6 ND grad.
June 2004

pages 68–9
1s at f22, 0.6 ND grad.
December 2005

pages 68–9
12s at f22, 0.9 ND grad, 0.3 ND grad.
January 2005

pages 70–1
Fotoman 617, 90mm Caltar lens. 1s at f22, 0.9
ND grad. February 2005

pages 72–3
3s at f22, 0.9 ND grad, polarizer.
January 2004

pages 74–5
20s at f32, 0.9 ND grad, 0.3 ND grad (staggered).
May 2004

pages 76–7
8s at f22, 0.3 ND grad.
May 2005

pages 76–7
1s at f22, 0.6 ND grad.
June 2004

pages 78–9
2s at f22, 0.6 ND grad.
May 2004

pages 80–1
4s at f22, 0.6 ND grad.
May 2004

page 82
1/2s at f22, 0.6 ND grad.
June 2004

page 83
25s at f22, 0.9 ND grad.
June 2005

page 83
1s at f22, 0.6 ND grad.
June 2005

pages 84–5
2s at f22, 0.9 ND grad.
June 2004

page 86
5s at f22, 0.3 ND grad, polarizer.
June 2005

page 86
2s at f32, 0.3 ND grad.
June 2005

pages 87
5s at f22, 0.6 ND grad.
June 2005

pages 88–9
Fotoman 617, 90mm Caltar lens, 12s at f32, 0.9
ND grad, 81c grad (inverted). March 2005

page 88
Fotoman 617, 90mm Caltar lens, 1s at f22, 0.9
ND grad. March 2005

pages 90–1
2s at f22, 0.9 ND grad.
June 2004

pages 92–3
9m at f16, unfiltered.
March 2004

page 93
90s at f16, unfiltered.
May 2005

pages 94–5
30s at f16, unfiltered.
March 2004

pages 94–5
5s at f32, 0.3 ND grad, 81c.
April 2005

pages 96–7
25s at f22, 0.6 ND grad (on side), 81ef.
July 2004

pages 98–9
20s at f22, 0.6 ND grard, 81d.
March 2004

page 99
20s at f32, 81ef.
March 2004

page 100–1
Fotoman 617, 90mm Caltar lens, 2s at f22, 0.6
ND grad, 81c. March 2005

pages 102–3
1/8s at f22, unfiltered.
September 2005

pages 102–3
10s at f16, unfiltered.
September 2005

pages 104–5
25s at f22, 0.6 ND grad.
December 2004

page 105
5s at f22, 0.9 ND grad.
December 2004

pages 106–7
1s at f22, 0.9 ND grad.
December 2005

page 108–9
1s at f16, 0.6 ND grad.
December 2005

pages 108–9
12s at f32, 0.6 ND grad.
December 2005

page 110
Fotoman 617, 90mm Caltar lens, 1s at f22, 0.6
ND grad. February 2005

page 110
1/4s at f16, 0.6 ND grad.
August 2005

page 111
1/2s at f22, 0.6 ND grad.
August 2005

pages 112–13
1/4s at f16, 0.6 ND grad.
August 2005

pages 114–15
5s at f32, 0.6 ND grad.
August 2005

pages 114–15
3s at f32, 0.6 ND grad, 81c.
October 2004

pages 116–17
3s at f32, 0.3 ND grad, 81c.
October 2004

page 117
1s at f22, 0.3 ND grad, 81c.
October 2004

ACKNOWLEDGMENTS

Mark Denton would like to thank the following who have helped directly in the making of this book:

Sir Alan Ayckbourn, Patrick Bongartz, Michael Brunström, Becky Clarke, Aynsley Cooper, Joe Cornish, Mike Denton, Rachel Denton, Paul Droluk, John Easby, Ian Edwards, Neil Harris, Bob Harvey, Matt & Jacqui Hough, Glynis & Mally Hunt, Liz Johnston, Colin Johnstone, Heidi Kipling, Pete Leeming, Anne Maidment, David Marshall, Graham Merritt, Anthony Mortimer, John Nichol, David Noton, Max Payne MBE, Gervase Phinn, Colin Prior, Dave Sallitt, Nicola Salvatore, Doug Segal, Ian & Tina Semple, Richard Stott, Carol Sutton, G.P. Taylor, Charlie Waite, David Ward, Steven Wignill.

Mark Denton's images are distributed by Panoramic Images Inc (Chicago) at www.panoramicimages.com and by www.markdentonphotographic.co.uk. Some images are used with kind permission of Panoramic Images Inc.

Limited edition prints of images from this book are available from www.markdentonphotographic.co.uk

For prints, postcards, commissions, photo sales and any other enquiries see www.markdentonphotographic.co.uk or contact Mark at markdentonphotographic@yahoo.co.uk and on 07709 905639.

Powerful seas can occur at any time of year. Here the pounding waves in July attack the cliffs to the west of Whitby. I was present to record the arrival of competitors in the Tall Ships race. Unfortunately the conditions were so poor that only three ships managed to reach Whitby; the others had to be diverted to safer ports.